Unfurling

Palewell Press

*Dear Pirg,
With Love from
Pirg. x*

Unfurling

poems as meditations and observances

Alison Lock

Unfurling - poems as meditations and observances
First edition 2022 from Palewell Press,
www.palewellpress.co.uk
Printed and bound in the UK

ISBN 978-1-911587-59-0

The cover design is Copyright © 2022 Camilla
Reeve
The cover image of a mandala was downloaded
from our image suppliers at
https://www.shutterstock.com/
The photo of Alison Lock on the back cover is
Copyright © 2022 Jean Bashford

A CIP catalogue record for this title is available
from the British Library.

Dedication

For Jilani

Introduction

I think of these poems as meditations, observances written during the many days of lockdown. Walking through the countryside near my home in the South Pennines was a time to unfold, seek solace, and release the negative thoughts and fear brought to us in the daily updates from the media. It was a time to engage deeply with the natural world from which I have always taken my inspiration.

At times, the imposed indoor life was stifling, but at least we were still able to connect with each other online. My meditation group, poetry, and other creative workshops continued to inspire me during the quiet days, and it was also an opportunity to try out new activities. Online platforms such as Zoom were, and still are, a way of stretching our networks far and wide. Finding new communities suddenly became possible. I joined in and became enamoured with the Dances of Universal Peace. The music from many traditions, the songs, and the accompanying dances are a beautiful form of body prayer, a nourishing way of expressing love from the heart, and a spiritual practice with its roots in Universal Sufism that is both joyful and nurturing.

During my daily walks, I became absorbed in the world around me, the minutiae that I might at other times have overlooked. I gathered these moments into my notebook, sensing the words until they flowed into one another, just like the days of this rare time of reflection. I hope this sequence will resonate with you and that you feel inspired by the natural wonders in your world, discovering as I have many precious moments of joy and hope.

Alison Lock

Meditations and Observances

i

What makes you feel alive?
      Is it the wingbeats of swans

whooping over the lake
      or the churr of a wren in a tree?

Are you made quiet
      in the awe of these wonders:

the blush of a rising sun,
      the white of an unknown day,

or the might of an endless sky?
      Do these things take your breath away?

Or is it a feather in the soothing hand of one
      who knows the secrets

of your tenderness, or the brush of silk
      against your cheek?

Do you open the window to breathe
      the aroma of newly laid tar?

Whatever awakens you,
      allow it to fill your being.

Take time to know the invisible plume,
      feel how you open and close and open again.

ii

Climb inside the warm place
    of your heart,

embrace all around,
    let petals surround you

as you walk in beauty.
    Breathe in,

breathe out,
    connect each step,

replenish
    with compassion.

iii

My eyes are drawn to you,
        tree with silver foliage.

I walk around you
        anticlockwise,

a slow unwinding
        – that's just my way.

I fold my arms around you.
        We hug.

Your skin has the attar
        of one steeped

in the heat of an ancient summer.
        As rain arrives,

I press my ear against you,
        listening to thirst.

iv

Within the hedge
    is a harbour

for the seeds of the fruit.
    On the lawn

is a hazel tree
    grown from a nut

planted by a squirrel.
    Acorns

in pools on the grit
    lulled by rain-tides.

Dormancy
    in still life.

7

V

Leaves tilt towards the bright light
      even in this dark season

where the air is sullied
      by the taint of indoor life.

Take a small cutting
      from below the node,

plant it among the clouds,
      water it with a river's kiss,

let it steep as you wait
      for drums to beat.

Ponder the air that slips
      between wavering stems.

Watch how the sepals hug
      the new-formed bud,

how time slows
      while

tendrils beckon
      across a tangled web.

vi

A goddess proffers
     her leafy palms,

opening her pores
     to the rain.

Her leaves are every shade
     of red:

crimson, cherry, cardinal,
     blood

filling each vein
     to the turning point

before the sun sets
     when there is still time to bloom.

vii

As the sun falls
    below the land

you are the eyes
    of Persephone.

Treasure
    the evening light

that defines
    the edge of night

in the geometric shadows
    of lamplight.

viii

In this wintering heart
    is the longing of an unspent year.

In this wintering heart
    I hold you tight.

In this wintering heart
    I flow around the shape of you.

In this wintering heart
    are all the unsaid words.

In this wintering heart
    tears wait to flow.

In this wintering heart
    is an ocean of love.

ix

Frost lacquers the fields,
    running a fine brush

along the top stones,
    bejewelling the walls.

To add to the glory,
    the sun glazes the land,

small flocks of goldfinch
    display improbable colours,

defying the sky
    with their chatter.

Snowdrops bow
    below green hoods,

their white petals
    a hope for peace.

X

Snow is falling
        on the hydrangeas,

once pink and blue,
        now white.

Snow is falling
        on the birdbath,

filling it with milk-white foam.
        Snow is falling

on the cat,
        freckling her winter coat.

Snow is falling
        on the ornamental statue

of the armless Venus,
        defenceless to the sky.

Snow slips
        between blades of grass.

Snow is the filigreed
        tracery of what remains.

xi

Be like the winter bracken
        on the moor.

Open your fronds to the snow,
        feel the deep chill.

Place your palms
        over your eyes,

look into the darkness
        of a world in pain.

This is how it is
        right now.

After dusk
        the nightjar flies.

xii

Drawing a green mantle
    over her shoulders,

Brigid sees the merle,
    hardly a speck in the sky,

she knows before long,
    the bird of Spring will arrive.

Taking an arrow from her sheaf,
    she dips it into the fire

draws her bow,
    unleashes a salutation.

Earth stirs from dreaming
    of warmer days

when Sarasvati's songs
    drift on a mountain draught.

The arrow lands as the ice melts
    – the first sign of Spring.

xiii

See the child's kite
　　up high in the sky.

Though it moves in the breeze,
　　let it be your focus.

See the world transformed,
　　filled with colour and flight.

xiv

When you skim
       a stone

across a lake,
       know that

all water
       aches

as it feels
       the quake.

XV

As you haul yourself
          up a steep bank of heather,

soil unpurls,
          roots dislodge.

You rest on the jutting rock,
          pleased you've climbed this far.

The valley below vibrates
          in snory dormancy

as if mesmerised
          by the slithering river.

All is quiet but for a shiver
          in the bracken

as a grouse rises.
          The horse in the next valley looks up

at the *ddddd* of a woodpecker
          in a distant tree.

Small birds sing under their wings,
          rocking your heart.

Beneath your foot
        a trodden nut parts

revealing the kernel of life
        of air, ground, water, light.

xvi

Rejoice in the unvoiced
    words of love.

Let them fly
    through the open window

until they form a cloak
    on the wings of birds.

Rest in the space
    between each breath.

xvii

Cygnets flap along
       the surface of the lake,

webbed feet trailing.
       Cob and pen look away.

I pick up a feather,
       its creamy colour

like the well-thumbed pages
       of a book,

the one by the telephone
       with its ink faded but legible.

I read all the names under S
       looking for a swan.

Many are silent shadows,
       others laid to rest

or simply dwell in a place
       beyond our hills,

but from these pages,
       they flicker back to life.

continued/

As I slip the feather
        into an unused pocket,

the one at the level of my heart,
        wings flutter.

Now, all they need
        is solid air

to perform the perfect grace,
        unfurling.

xviii

Close your lips,
       listen to your heart

as you watch the eclipse
       of the moon.

Feel the cool of its shine
       warm your soul

as the unspooled light
       illuminates the night,

leaving a trace
       in the stars.

xix

You stare at the lake
    you know so well,

but the lake says:
    'Walk away,

forget me,
    my history, my name,

or how I have sprung from the earth
    or travelled

from the hills,
    puddling, whirling, pooling.

Now look again,
    see me afresh,

re-remember the first time
    you saw me,

the first breath you took
    at the conscious sight of me.'

XX

Feel the heat
    of the ancient sun

in its infinite space.
    Conjure a fig tree

from the flames of the fire.
    Let your heart

sing out loud
    so it may be heard

in the places where others meet.
    Eat, pray, dance.

xxi

Fill your bowl
      to the brim,

enjoy a carnival
      of strawberries,

taste the Lammas loaf.
      Share the harvest

of the sun,
      all its divine ripeness.

xxii

A cloud of silver
      is the gentle knowing

that arrives
      as a feather in flight.

Open your crown
      to the shower of light,

feel new wings
      lift your desire

to fly like a heron
      across the lake.

Be a starling
      up high in the sky,

the tiny speck within
      a murmuration.

xxiii

The swans' long necks
      sway in synchronicity

as they land
      on the other side of the lake.

xxiv

You find yourself
     on your knees

marvelling
     at the silk of a worm cast,

tracing the silver trails
     of a slug,

curious at the shape
     left by a caterpillar's mouth.

Treat all with mercy,
     let kindness grow.

XXV

Even the air breathes.
    I've heard it billow

among the standing trees,
    low and hoarse

it skims a chorus
    through unfurnished branches,

playing top notes
    among catkins,

trilling wing-like
    through holly, gorse, and broom.

Rocks and boulders
    answer with a sigh.

xxvi

Breathe in the sun
      exhale the moon.

Find the cool
      on the lee side,

the warmth
      from the bright jewel.

Be aware
      of the shadows

in the stillness
      of your heart.

xxvii

You long for your origins,
　　　always seeking

the source,
　　　but you only see branches,

broken lines,
　　　like a language in code.

Reach for the mother tree,
　　　the well-spring of life,

see the seed
　　　from which we all grew.

xxviii

As Mabon's wheel of fire
    crosses the sky,

there's a second crop
    of orange hawkweed,

a blaze of spokes
    from the flame of the hub.

Enjoy the sun
    of yellow petals,

small mirrors
    reflected in light.

Do not think of fading
    as the end of summer

but as nourishment
    for another year.

Allow yourself
    to absorb each ray.

xxix

You say life has no purpose,
        but look at your hands.

When you try to scrub them clean
        there remains

a trace of dough,
        the staff that keeps you whole,

and on the heels of your hands
        are blisters

from digging the soil,
        the essence of clay

caught in your lifeline
        as you form a vessel

to describe a thousand stars.
        See how they fall and rise,

a kinesis of dust,
        motes in sunlight.

xxx

When you dance
    in starlit fields,

seek the stillness
    at the centre

of the mandala.
    Let all else spin.

Stay awhile in the calm
    of the bloom.

xxxi

As the doors of the darkest night
    are opened

the Samhain candles are lit.
    Chant, sing, ululate,

as Persephone
    returns to the earth,

soil crumbles,
    prisms of quartz glow,

leaves are released
    from their trees,

the dead are riffled
    by the breeze.

xxxii

By St Dwynwen's cross
     you stand at the edge

of a nascent world
     where seas embrace.

Breathe in
     until your lungs are filled

with the essence
     of those who are alive

and all who have died.
     Their breath

and yours
     is in the murmuring hum

of every wounded spirit
     waiting to be healed.

xxxiii

You are at the centre
        of the labyrinth.

All these words
        are chants

forever seeking
        the ways of perfection.

Let them form tales
        to nurture your heart.

Acknowledgements

Thank you to those who shared my shrunken world during the restrictions of lockdown. To Ian and Lewin for their steadfast support; to Jean, Stacey, and Julie, for their wisdom and friendship; to Jilani and Salik for bringing many of us together across the oceans; to Mary for her encouragement and kind comments; to editor Camilla Reeve for believing in this project; and, if I could, I would thank every creature, tree, hillside, lake, river, and the many manifestations of sky for all the inspiration and quiet revealing of the ever-beating heart of life.

Alison Lock - Biography

Alison Lock is the author of two short story collections, four collections of poetry, and a novella, as well as contributor to several anthologies and reviews. She is a tutor for Transformative Life Writing courses and has an MA in Literature Studies and Creative Writing. Her poetry collections are *A Slither of Air (2011), Beyond Wings (2015), Revealing the Odour of Earth (2017)*, and *Lure (2020)* – a poetic sequence of personal transformation broadcast on BBC Radio 3. She was Poet in Residence at Holmfirth Arts Festival 2012 and opened the 2013 Festival with her evocative *Eye of the Heron.* Her short story collections are *Above the Parapet (2013)*, and *A Witness of Waxwings (2017)*. Her stories have won prizes including: The London Magazine Short Story Competition 2014, The Sentinel Quarterly Review, The 14th Conference for the Short Story in English at Shanghai, the Segora5 International Short Story Prize 2020. Her work was nominated for the Pushcart Prize 2020. www.alisonlock.com

Palewell Press

Palewell Press is an independent publisher handling poetry, fiction and non-fiction with a focus on books that foster Justice, Equality and Sustainability. The Editor can be reached on enquiries@palewellpress.co.uk